D0581925

THE **BATMAN** MOVIE

BATMAN'S GUIDE TO BEING COOL

BY HOWIE DEWIN

Photos ©: 75 bikes: Kittisak_Taramas/Thinkstock; 75 skates: Dorling Kindersley/Thinkstock; 75 skis: incomible/Thinkstock; 75 scooters: Xpdream/Dreamstime; 75 skateboards: AlexanderYershov/Thinkstock; 75 sneakers: neyro2008/Thinkstock.

Scholastic Children's Books
Euston House,
24 Eversholt Street,
London NW1 1DB, UK

A division of Scholastic Ltd
London ~ New York ~ Toronto ~ Sydney ~ Auckland
Mexico City ~ New Delhi ~ Hong Kong

This book was first published in the US in 2017 by Scholastic Inc.
Published in the UK by Scholastic Ltd, 2017

HARDBACK EDITION ISBN 978 1407 17729 8
SCHOLASTIC CLUBS AND FAIRS EDITION 978 1407 17992 6

Book design by Jessica Meltzer

2 4 6 8 10 9 7 5 3

Printed in the UK by CPI Group (UK) Ltd, Croydon, CR0 4YY

MIX
Paper from
responsible sources
FSC® C020471

CONTENTS

ARE YOU READY TO HANG WITH

BATMAN

AND LEARN A FEW

LIFE LESSONS

ALONG THE WAY?

INTRODUCTION

CONGRATULATIONS! You just got lucky. You have been chosen to learn how to be Mega-Cool.

Being Mega-Cool is not the same as being the ordinary, normal kind of cool. Why? Because I'm Batman and I said so!

You see, I radiate Mega-Cool. I exude it. And so do my awesome, Mega-Cool friends. (You'll meet them in just a minute.)

Being Mega-Cool means you know how to save the city, the country and the planet – with some help from your Mega-Cool friends, of course.

It means you stalk the night, fight crime and rap like a heavy-metal machine. It means you know how to dress and talk and arrive with a Mega-Cool, cowl-wearing kind of style. It means you will get to use the Mega-Coolest gadgets and gear in the universe!

And it means YOU are going to learn directly from ME how to be the coolest person in the world. (My cool friends might throw in some tips along the way.)

Yep. You're going to learn to be Mega-Cool. You're welcome.

You'll be in good company.

ME AND MY SON/SIDEKICK, ROBIN.

STAY BY MY SIDE. WE'RE ABOUT TO DO SOME SERIOUS SUPER-HERO SIDEKICK STUFF.

MR. WAYNE, DO YOU THINK YOU'D BE INTERESTED IN ADOPTING ME AS YOUR FUTURE ORPHAN SON?

DEFINITELY.

AND THIS IS MY MEGA-COOL ALTER EGO, BILLIONAIRE BRUCE WAYNE, WITH HIS ADOPTED SON, DICK.

I'm lucky to have such Mega-Cool people who want to hang out with me...

ME WITH ALFRED, MY OLDEST FRIEND AND FATHER FIGURE.

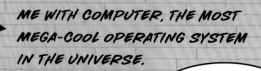

ME WITH COMPUTER, THE MOST
MEGA-COOL OPERATING SYSTEM
IN THE UNIVERSE.

HEY, COMPUTER!
I'M HOME!

WELCOME HOME, SIR.
INITIALISING BATCAVE
OPERATING SYSTEM.

BATMAN'S GUIDE TO

DISCOVERING YOUR
INNER COOL

The first thing I want to say to you is this: it takes time to find your Inner Cool. I hope you don't think I got *this cool* overnight. No way! It's taken a long time, plus a lot of practice with my heroic crime-fighting moves.

Yes, I've been living large, 24/7, 365, at a million per cent, since way before you were born. So don't worry if you don't feel like Batman overnight. Great things are worth the wait! And it's GREAT to be Batman.

Trust me, I know.

Because I am... **BATMAN**!

(I just love saying that!)

The truth is, the search for your Inner Cool starts right now – and it will continue for the rest of your life! Finding your Inner Cool means that every day you vow to:

- USE YOUR SUPERPOWERS FOR GOOD.
- ONLY DO WHAT IS DECENT.
- ALWAYS SHOW UP AND HELP WHERE YOU ARE NEEDED.
- ALWAYS MAKE TIME FOR YOUR MEGA-COOL FRIENDS.

So turn the page and start finding out exactly what kind of cool you are!

WHAT'S YOUR COOL SUPERPOWER?

Superpowers come in all different shapes and sizes. It's VERY important to stay true to whatever your superpower is. Don't ever think your powers aren't important enough to make the world a better place! You are the ONLY one who can be the Super Hero you were born to be. So make sure you take care of your superpower and develop it.

Be on the lookout as you try different things – doing a maths problem, kicking a ball, baking cookies, taking care of your dog, writing a poem. There are so many different kinds of superpowers. You have to keep trying new things to find yours!

What's your cool style?
Wear your style with confidence. I'm Batman and I say you look good!

WHAT'S YOUR COOL MISSION?

Once you figure out your superpower, you'll come one step closer to figuring out your mission.

Of course, there are all different kinds of missions – some are small and some are big. Here are a few examples:

DAILY

- FEED THE DOG
- DO YOUR HOMEWORK
- CLEAN YOUR ROOM
  (Some people don't consider this a daily mission.)

YEARLY

- **DO WELL AT SCHOOL**
- **JOIN A SPORTS TEAM OR ACT IN A PLAY**
- **CLEAN YOUR ROOM**

  (For those of you who think of this as more of an annual thing.)

LIFETIME

- **KEEP HUMANKIND SAFE FROM CRIME AND DESTRUCTION** (No big deal. All in a day's work.)

IF YOU HAPPEN TO BE BATMAN... WHICH I AM! HAVE I MENTIONED? I SOOOO LOVE SAYING THAT.

So take on all the missions that are set before you, big and small. It's the best way to really develop your superpowers!

What's your cool symbol?
It's good to have a symbol. I highly recommend creating your own symbol. I use this. Note how it reflects my *style*. It's sleek and chic and it never goes out of fashion.

YOU WANT TO GET NUTS?

COME ON.

LET'S GET NUTS.

PLAYLISTS

Gym Workout

Super Cool Mega Mix

LET'S GET NUTS Mix

Batman Solos

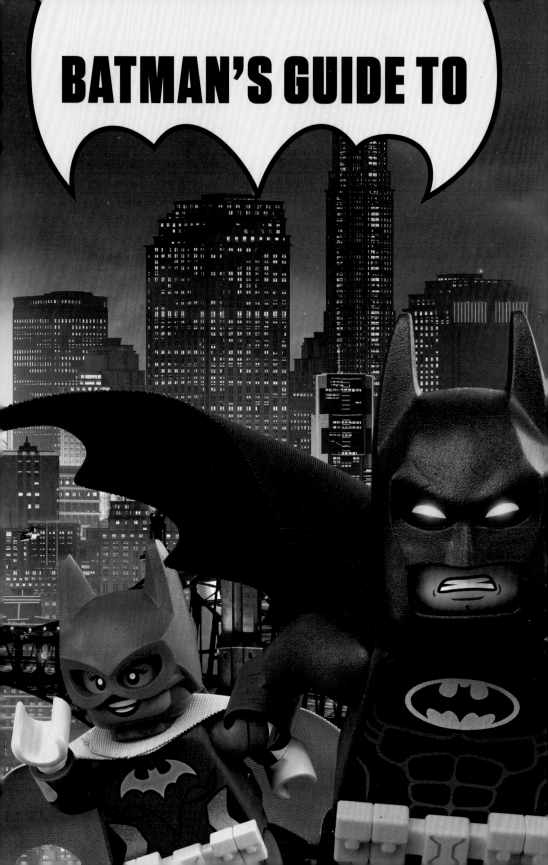

BATMAN'S GUIDE TO

MEETING MEGA-COOL FRIENDS

WHEN IT COMES TO FINDING MEGA-COOL FRIENDS, YOU HAVE TO ASK YOURSELF A FEW IMPORTANT QUESTIONS.

DO YOU SPEAK THE SAME LANGUAGE?

This doesn't mean Spanish, English, French or Chinese. It means, when you're talking to your friends, do you get that cool feeling that they understand *exactly* what you mean?

And, of course, it works both ways, too. Although if you happen to be Batman (which I AM!), then you say really important stuff all the time. So it's extra-important that your friends understand that!

YOU READY TO DO SOMETHING COOL?

YEAH! ALWAYS!

DO YOU HAVE COMMON INTERESTS?

If you are a crime-fighting vigilante, then it's good if your friends like to fight crime, too.

DO YOU HANG OUT IN THE SAME PLACES?

If you're going to be spending a lot of time zooming around to exotic locations to find the criminals you were born to defeat, then it's good if your friends are visiting those places, too. Or if you spend your downtime swimming in your pool, then it's good if one of your best friends is a dolphin.

ME AND MY GOOD FRIEND DOLPHY.

Take a peek at me hanging out with my friends. We have so much in common...

ALFRED: Tail gunner for the Royal Air Force. Considers taking care of BATMAN the most important job in the world. I can't argue.

BARBARA GORDON: Hotshot pilot. Graduate of Harvard for Police. Likes wearing headgear with ears. It's a good look; I'm not gonna lie.

DICK GRAYSON: Orphan. Nimble gymnast. Wants to grow up to be just like BATMAN! And how could that be wrong?

DOLPHY: Loves swimming... and me, BATMAN! Let's be honest, who doesn't?

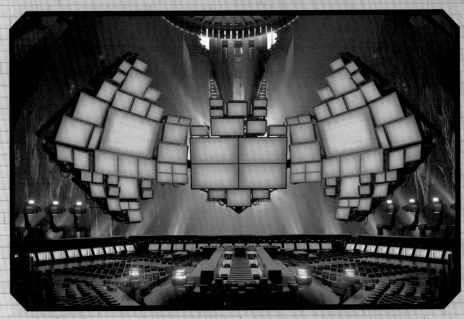

COMPUTER: Knows everything! What could be more like ME than that?! Talk about having stuff in common!

We definitely have common interests...

... WE SPEAK THE SAME LANGUAGE!

Here's a quick guide to the lingo my team and I use:

WORD	MEANING
Boom!	Common remark after a stealthy move
Kaboom!	Common remark after a mega-stealthy move
Pow!	Sound heard after deploying a Mega-Cool gadget
Woo-hoo!	Celebratory remark after discovering that one of your dads is Batman

MY DREAM IS FOR THE POLICE FORCE TO TEAM UP WITH BATMAN.

BATMAN'S GUIDE TO

DEFEATING YOUR ENEMIES

I used to say that Batman likes to battle lots of villains. I didn't have a number-one bad guy. And I didn't have any number-one friends, either.

You see, for a long time, I believed in working solo. But that changed when I met my Batman family. I finally started to get the hang of this team thing.

And that's when I realised that the Joker was right about one thing (just the one) – he really *is* my number-one bad guy.

Now don't get me wrong – I'm still a night-stalking, crime-fighting vigilante and a heavy-metal rapping machine. But I have to say one thing about the Joker: he makes me bring my A-game.

But just because I have one greatest enemy doesn't mean I don't know my other enemies. You can't be a hugely successful, world-famous, crime-fighting legend without knowing all about your enemies' strengths.

Mr. Freeze
"I freeze things!"

IT'S ALWAYS GOOD TO DRESS IN LAYERS WHEN FIGHTING CRIME.

Poison Ivy
"I control plants."

COMPUTER CAN FORMULATE A REALLY TOXIC WEEDKILLER!

The Penguin
"I can talk to flightless, aquatic birds."

PENGUINS ARE MY LEAST FAVOURITE MOVIE ANIMALS.

Two-Face
"I make unpredictable decisions."

I PREDICT THE UNPREDICTABLE!

Bane
"I smash things."

I'M A MASTER BUILDER! I FIX THINGS!

The Riddler
"I confuse people!"

YOU CAN'T STUMP ME!

Harley Quinn
"I love helping my puddin' come up with plans!"

AND I LOVE FOILING THEIR PLANS OVER AND OVER AGAIN!

The Joker

"I do art comedy!"

YOU DO CRAZY!

These guys don't scare me because I also know their weaknesses... which... in every case is... wait for it... yes, you know it...

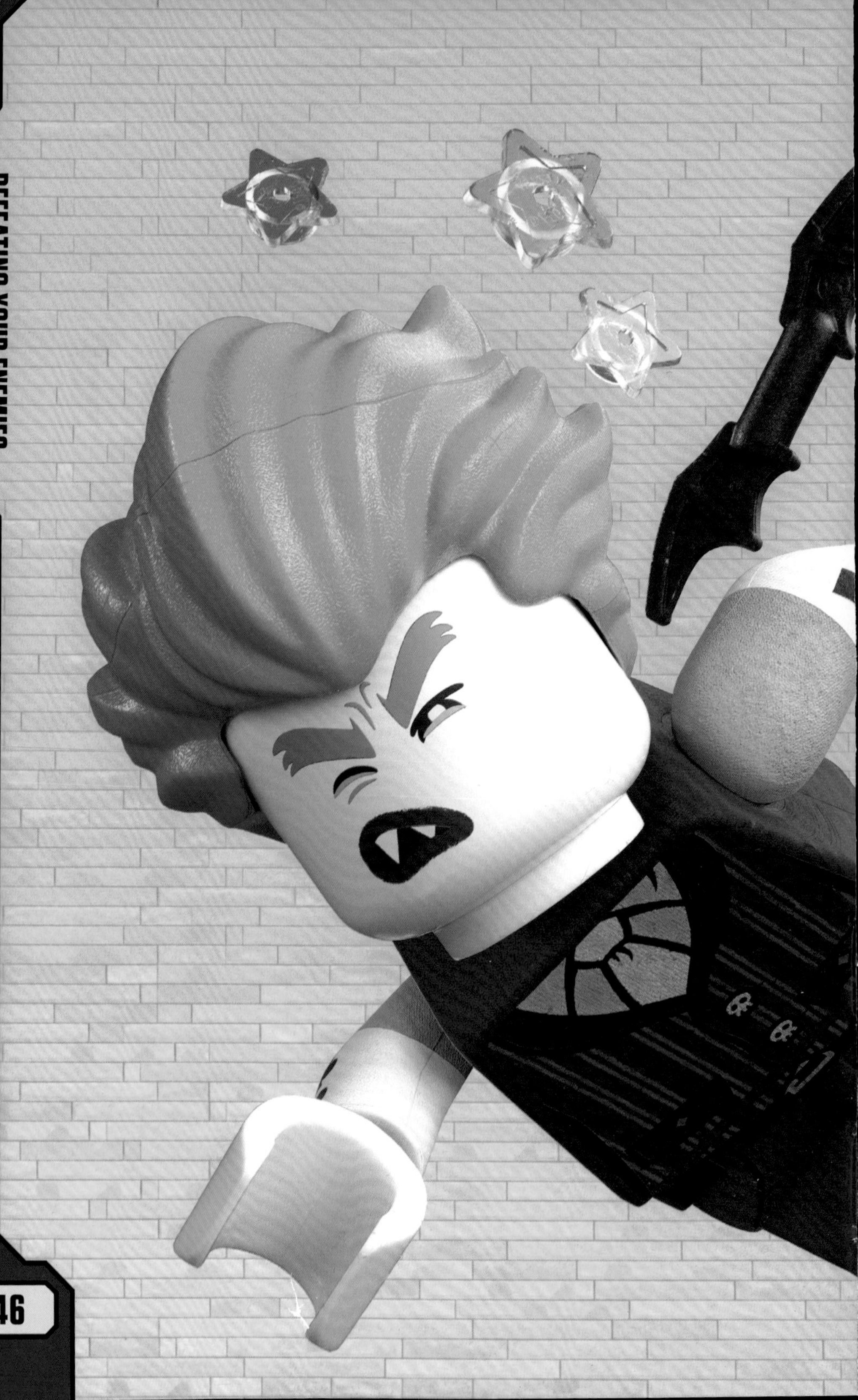

ME! BATMAN!

I'VE GOT A **SURPRISE** FOR YOU AND IT'S GOING TO MAKE YOU **SMILE!**

MAKING A MEGA-COOL IMPRESSION

There's more to being Mega-Cool than hanging with your awesome friends, saving the planet together.

Sure, I'll admit it, you have to be able to walk (or zoom or screech or zap) into any situation and be ready to take down six (or eight or ten or twelve) super-villains all at once.

But if you don't have exactly the right gear for the job, then you really aren't doing it in Batman style.

So check out your wardrobe. Make sure you know exactly what you'll use and wear, no matter which criminal mastermind you're about to face.

And remember, whatever the outfit, you have to wear it with total confidence. Being Mega-Cool means knowing you look GOOD!

By the way, this is not a mask I'm wearing. It's an armoured face disguise in the shape of the animal criminals fear most. *That's* what I'm talkin' about!

SURPRISES!

No crime-fighting plan is complete without a few good surprises! When it comes to springing out on villains, I'm a master of stealth! Just look how I surprised the Joker and Mayor McCaskill!

TIP:
One of the best things about surprising people is using disguises. But the trickiest part of any disguise is hiding your individual swagger. It's all about finding the right balance between swagger and surprise.

EXTREME CONDITIONS!

Just because you have to travel across the globe to fight crime doesn't mean you have to lose your Mega-Cool style. You can be 50,000 leagues under the sea or 50 degrees below zero and still feel *gooooood!*

TIP:
Don't be afraid to share your Mega-Cool gear and gadgets!

HERE'S DICK HAVING A LITTLE FUN WITH MY MEGA-COOL GET-UPS!

GLAM

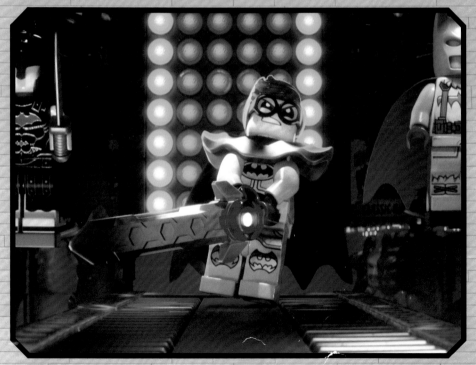

KNIGHT

CLAWS

SILENT BUT DEADLY

WINGS

TIP:
It's okay to have fun
while you fight crime.
Just ask Dick.

FLAMES

ON THE TOWN!

Don't let anyone tell you that dress-up clothes aren't cool. How could you possibly not be in the mood to party when you're looking this fine? You will be the hit of every party, like me and my boy, Dick!

CLASSIC TUXEDO LOOK

KISSY FACE

THE BAD BOY

What's your cool style?
It's important to know the right poses for the right outfit. Look what you can do with one tuxedo!

THE ALTER EGO!

I'm not saying I have one, but if you do happen to have an alter ego, make sure he or she looks as good as you do!

BRUCE WAYNE

Billionaire!
Bon vivant!
Gallivanter!

Gotham City's Most Eligible Bachelor for, like, ninety years in a row!

TIP:
An alter ego should get to have just as much fun as you do.

CALL ME
BRUCE, CHAMP!

Phone!

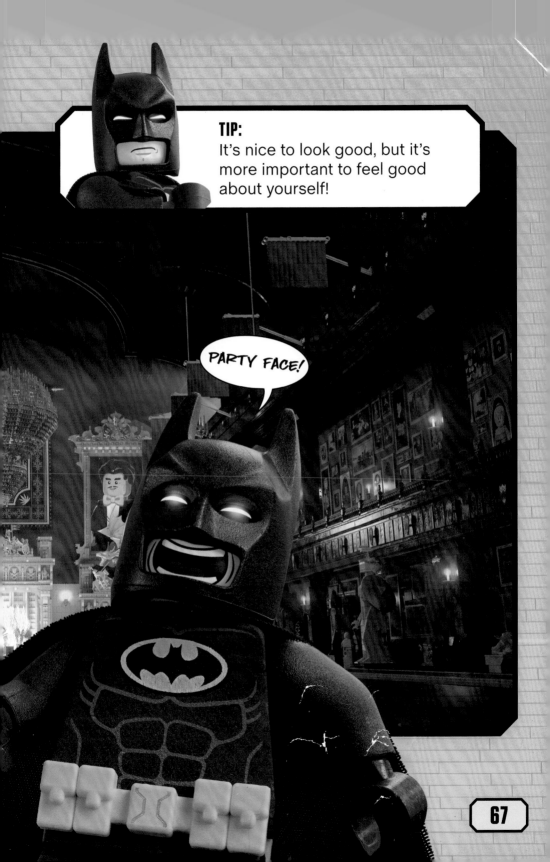

TIP:
It's nice to look good, but it's more important to feel good about yourself!

PARTY FACE!

THE COMPANY YOU KEEP!

Let's be honest here... I am Batman, and I look good no matter where I go, what I'm doing or who I'm with.

    But I have to take my hat off to my friends. They know how to look good too! Check out my friends sporting some Mega-Cool threads.

ALFRED
aka Alfred

DICK GRAYSON
aka Robin

TIP: Don't forget to compliment your friends when you see them looking as good as you do!

BARBARA GORDON
aka Batgirl

BATMAN'S GUIDE TO

ARRIVING IN MEGA-COOL STYLE

"The Speedwagon"

When you get the call that it's time to save the day, it's mega-important to be ready! You have to have the right vehicle at the right time for the right job.

Here's a tip. Whatever you happen to be driving, put your symbol on it. Remember how I told you to create your own symbol? Here's why: anything you put your symbol on gets cooler and cooler. Pretty soon, it doesn't really matter what you arrive in. As long as it's got your symbol on it, *everything* is cool!

I'll show you a few examples of what I mean.

GOT IT? NOW GO PUT YOUR SYMBOL ON SOME STUFF AND MAKE IT COOL!

WHO CARES?   MEGA-COOL!

Bike

Bike!

Skates!

Skates!

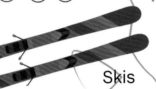

Skis

Skis

Scooter

Scooter!

Skateboard

Skateboard!

Shoes

Shoes!

VEHICLES

Here are just a few of the sweet rides I keep safe and sound in the Batcave.

BATMOBILE

Terrain: Open road
Speed: Whatever is necessary
Manoeuvrability: EXTREME

BATMAN ZEPPELIN

Terrain: Lower airspace
Speed: Super Hero sedate
Manoeuvrability: Straight up, straight down, straight sideways

BATMAN SUB

Terrain: Under water
Speed: Faster than Dolphy
Manoeuvrability: Better than a shark

BATMAN SPACE SHUTTLE

Terrain: The cosmos
Speed: Supersonic
Manoeuvrability: Orbits like a dream

SCUTTLER

Terrain: Streets. Walls. Sky. Pretty much anywhere and everywhere
Speed: Like a quick-change artist
Manoeuvrability: Anywhere. Anytime. "Forwards" and "backwards" are not in the Scuttler's vocabulary

BATMAN KAYAK

Terrain: Rapids
Speed: Faster than the river
Manoeuvrability: Upside down and inside out in seconds flat

BATWING

Terrain: Sky
Speed: Classified
Manoeuvrability: Classified

YOU DON'T NEED STATISTICS TO KNOW THAT THIS IS ONE COOL RIDE!!!
I'LL SAY JUST ONE THING... VERTICAL TAKE-OFF.
SWEET!

SOMETIMES, THE BEST WAY TO **GET WHAT YOU WANT** IS TO ACT LIKE **YOU DON'T WANT IT AT ALL.**

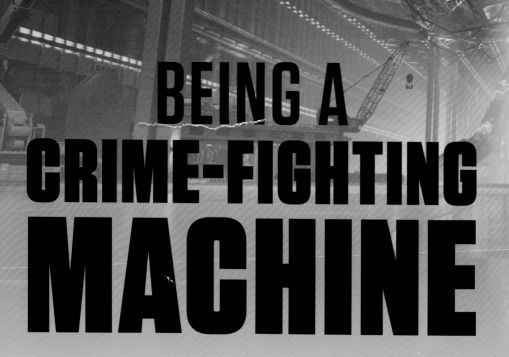

BATMAN'S GUIDE TO

BEING A
CRIME-FIGHTING
MACHINE

I used to think a real Super Hero should know how to handle the bad guys without backup. It's not wrong to have help, but it just wasn't the Batman way.

That changed when I met my friends. My butler, Alfred, who's a mentor and father figure. My son, Dick Grayson. And Barbara Gordon, Gotham City's mega-smart police commissioner.

So now I have these Mega-Cool friends to help me fight crime. Together, we are the ultimate crime-fighting machine!

Obviously, we have all the right skills to be extremely cool Super Heroes. You know what I'm talking about – flying, leaping, climbing tall buildings, Master Building Mega-Cool things, lightning speed, devastating good looks.

But! We need more than that. To be Super Heroes, we also have to have all the right gear!

Don't tell anyone I told you this, but... a Super Hero is not a Super Hero without the cool gadgets.

If you tell anyone I said that, I will deny it.

But take a look at what I mean...

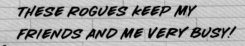

THESE ROGUES KEEP MY FRIENDS AND ME VERY BUSY!

ELECTRONICS!

NO GADGETS

LESS COOL

GADGETS

MORE COOL

Tip: Always be on the lookout for the Bat-Signal!

ELECTRONICS!

NO GADGETS

LESS COOL

GADGETS

MORE COOL

TOOLS OF THE TRADE!

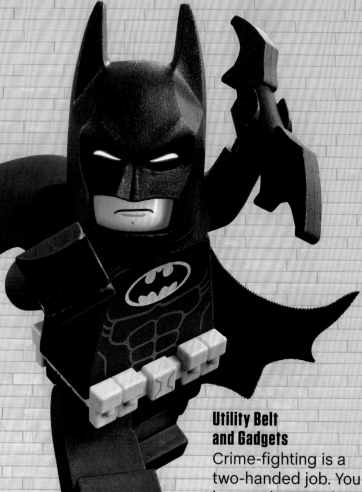

Utility Belt and Gadgets

Crime-fighting is a two-handed job. You have to have a place to store your tools while you're fighting the crime!

Batarangs

Your weapon will always come back for more, but your enemies won't!

Good Idea Tracker

It's always a good idea to be able to keep track of your brilliance.

GOOD IDEAS TRACKER
BATMAN
5,678,483
EVERYONE ELSE
0

SHARING IS CARING!

Batman Bucks
When Batman gives you Batman bucks, use them to buy Mega-Cool stuff for you and your friends to share!

"The Speedwagon"

Merch Gun

So you've perfected your symbol and put it on a bunch of stuff. Great! But what good is all that stuff if you don't have friends to share it with?

THE ULTIMATE GADGET!

Some relationships are complicated. But something about Computer just lets me relax. It's a toy, a gadget, a tool, a weapon... a friend.

COMPUTER, OVERCOMPENSATE!

I'M ON MY WAY, SIR!

The Joker: It's only a matter of time before I take over Gotham City.
Batman: When has that ever happened? Computer?
Computer: Never.

What could be better?

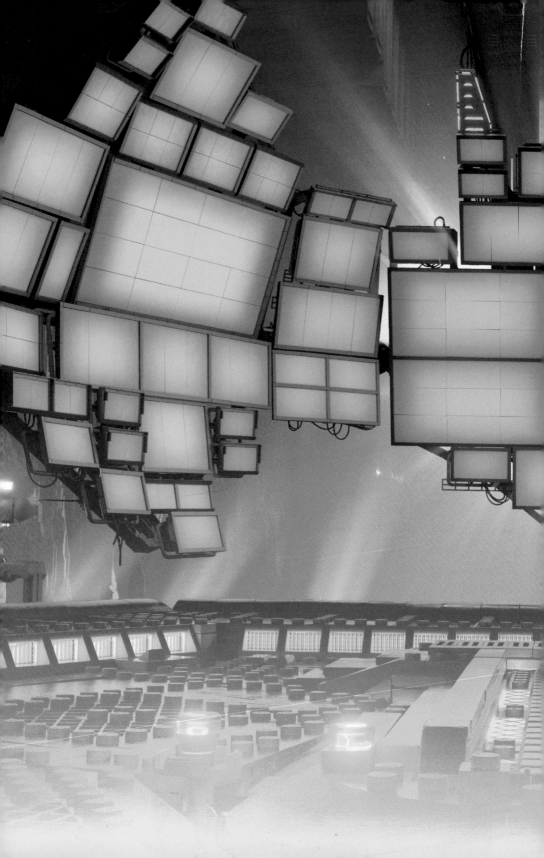

BATMAN'S GUIDE TO

I'M ABOUT TO GIVE YOU AN INCREDIBLY IMPORTANT TIP:

RELAX.

Even Super Heroes need downtime.
The ultimate way to prove how cool you are
is to make sure you know how to chill!
Personally, I like to do it all in the comfort of
my own remarkably cool home.
(Wow. That was exhausting. Good thing I'm
about to relax.)

GO SHOPPING IN YOUR OWN CLOSET.

PLAY DRESS-UP WITH
YOUR FRIENDS.

TELL A JOKE.

Why do Super Heroes love jokes?
Because there's always a *punch*line!

ENJOY A GOURMET MEAL – IN YOUR OWN KITCHEN.

GO SWIMMING WITH FRIENDS.

TELL A JOKE.

Why did Alfred give Batman a mint?
Because he had bat breath!

VISIT MUSEUMS – ESPECIALLY ONES DEDICATED TO YOURSELF.

**SPEND TIME HANGING
OUT WITH YOUR
MEGA-COOL FRIENDS.**

TELL A JOKE.

**What position did
Bruce Wayne play on
his cricket team?**
Batsman!

MASTER BRUCE, YOU LIVE ON AN ISLAND FIGURATIVELY AND LITERALLY. YOU CAN'T SPEND THE REST OF YOUR LIFE ALONE, DRESSED IN BLACK, LISTENING TO LOUD MUSIC AND STAYING UP ALL NIGHT.

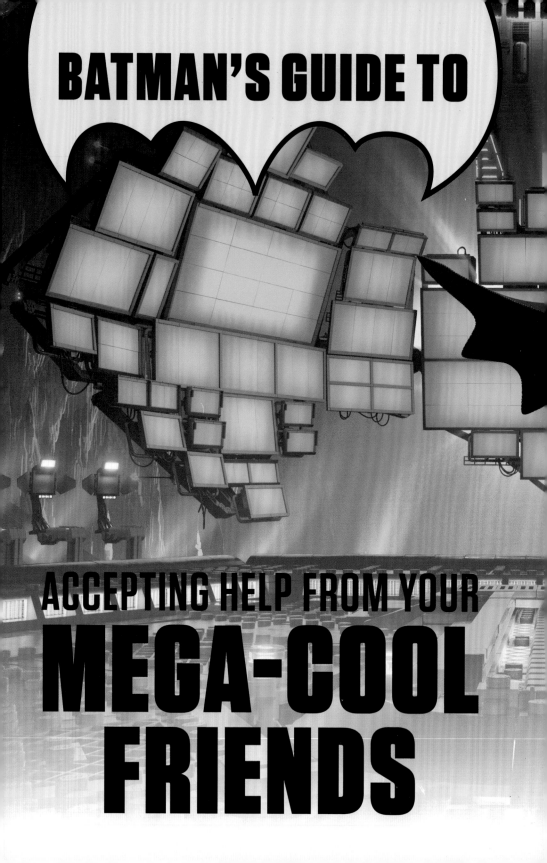

Okay. Time for true confessions. It's not easy for a Super Hero like me to admit this, but... things do go a bit better when I work together with my friends.

It's true. I have friends.

Now, I'm not saying I *can't* conquer every bad guy in the world all by myself. I'm just saying sometimes it's a teeny bit easier... and a lot more fun... when I don't do it alone.

So, here are the five questions this Super Hero asks when it comes to figuring out which friends I can count on when the going gets tough.

1. AM I CLOSE WITH THIS PERSON?
2. DOES THIS PERSON HAVE MY BACK?
3. DO I SHARE MY THINGS WITH THIS PERSON?
4. DO I STAY WITH THIS PERSON WHEN THINGS GET TOUGH?
5. DO I TRUST THIS PERSON?

Try out these questions on your own friends. If you answer YES to all the questions, then you know you have a Super Hero of a friend! (And you also know your Super-Hero friend is Batman Approved!)

HERE ARE SOME WAYS YOU CAN LET FRIENDS KNOW HOW IMPORTANT THEY ARE.

DO THINGS TOGETHER.

NOW I'M FREE, NOW I'M GROOVIN', COME ON, BATMAN, LET'S GET MOVIN'!

FAREWELL!

CONGRATULATIONS! You have completed the first very important steps to becoming three incredibly great things:

1) **MEGA-COOL**
2) **YOUR OWN SUPER HERO**
3) **A BATMAN-APPROVED FRIEND**

Now, come on! Go ahead. Say, "Thank you, Batman!" Because how many Super Heroes could give you ALL THAT in one book?

I'll admit it. I'm impressed with myself.

But enough about me...

I'm pretty impressed with you, too. So whaddaya say you put all this incredibly great advice I've given you to work?

MAKE SURE YOUR VERSION OF "COOL" MEANS:

- YOU ALWAYS STAND UP FOR WHAT'S RIGHT.
- YOU ALWAYS STAND UP TO BULLIES AND DEFEND THE LITTLE GUY.
- YOU ALWAYS MAKE THE HERO MOVE.
- YOU ALWAYS FIND WAYS TO MAKE THE TOUGH WORK FUN.
- YOU ALWAYS TREAT YOUR FRIENDS LIKE THE SUPER HEROES THEY ARE.

If you do all that, then you won't just be a Super Hero. You will be *my* hero!

Good luck and see you soon!

- BATMAN

EVERYBODY SAY FAMILY!

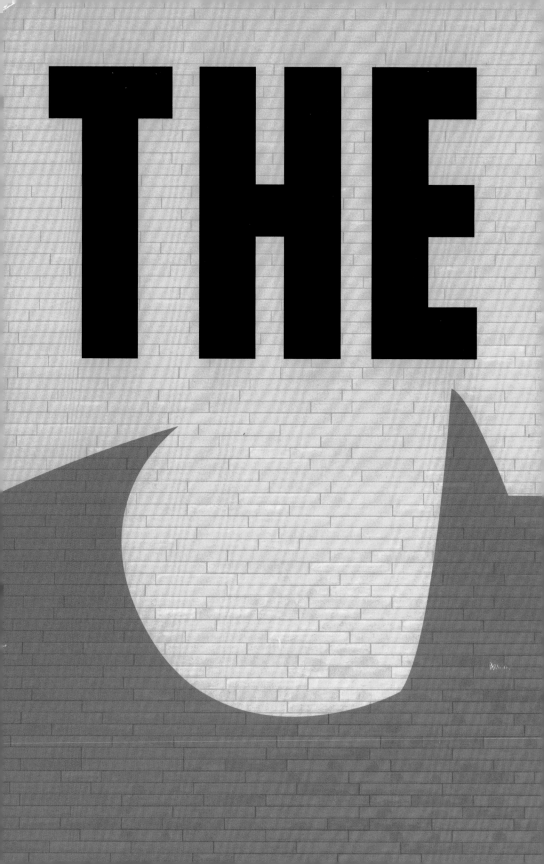